# HERCULES IS AN ASSHOLE

# AN ODE TO THE MEN OF MYTHOLOGY WHO SUCK, AND TO THE WOMEN OF MYTHOLOGY WHO SUFFERED

## Shaelyn Fisher

BookLeaf Publishing

India | USA | UK

Presentation by *BookLeaf Publishing*

Web: www.bookleafpub.com

E-mail: info@bookleafpub.com

ISBN: 9789358739077

First edition 2021

# DEDICATION

To all of the Herculeses, Zeuses, and Poseidons of this world wondering if this poem is about them- LOL yup, it absolutely is. Turns out that spite is one hell of a motivator! You probably should have behaved better, huh? ;)

To all of the Medusas of this world- you are made of stone and scales and divinity. He will never be enough to break you. Don't ever forget your own power.

# PREFACE

The world may call them heroes, but us monsters know the truth: a hero needs a monster to slay before they can be called heroic.

By what name do we call the ones who create monsters?

Remember this, Darling- no one blames the Ocean when sailors drown at sea.

# ACKNOWLEDGMENT

There is not nearly enough ink in my pen to thank everyone that I need to, but I've never been a quitter so I'll give it my very best try!

To my family, who have admirably tolerated my tendency towards months of silence before randomly shoving a poem at them for approval before quickly retreating into more silence- your patience with my moody tendencies and your unwavering support of my poetry (even though poetry is not really your cup of tea!) is more appreciated than I know how to express. I love you all very much. When I learn how to write love poems, I will write them for you.

To my inner circle- you know who you are, and you know I could not have done it without you. You guys perform the "hype friend" role like its your actual paid job, and I am so grateful for the encouragement, without which I would never have been brave enough to let these poems see the light of day. I've always had the courage of a field mouse, but you ladies taught me the bravery I only ever read about.

And to anyone who reads these poems and can relate to them: You are divine, you are worthy of love, and you are enough. Astra inclinant, sed non obligant. Screw the stars. Write your own damn story.

# 1. SEX BEFORE MARRIAGE

Mama, tell that preacher man that sex wasn't the sin here- it was the serpent slithering unwelcome into the Garden. There should have been consent involved in consuming the apple.

No, Adam, coercion is not consent; your Father should have taught you that.

If a man's hands are dirty enough to defile you at his touch, don't you think he has more to be praying about than you do? After all, only one of us was made from dust.

## 2. ATHENA SPEAKS OF MEDUSA

I didn't create Medusa, Poseidon. Your hands on her body were toxic.

What were you thinking, dragging her to my temple? Touching while she begged you to stop?

But what mortal can fight off a god? What did you think would happen when the saltwater on your skin corroded her innocence?

The snakes I gave her were meant for her protection. It was your actions that hardened her gaze to stone.

# 3. HAVE A GLASS OF WINE AND TELL ME A STORY

My trauma ages like a fine wine. That is to say, I don't bottle my pain, I barrel it.

What I mean is I put it all in a wooden cask and bury it deep in my chest next to my lungs where it is colder and darker and I let it ferment for years until I pour it in a glass and gulp it down like cyanide or arsenic or the finest vintage red that you've ever tasted.

Sometimes I think being so close to my lungs causes it to oxidize too early and every time I find myself unable to breathe I end up with sour vinegar. Sometimes I vomit my feelings and then the acidity tastes off. Sometimes it ages well, and I can sip on it for hours. Sometimes I can smell notes of that cologne I loved or taste hints of a first kiss and if I gently stir the glass I can even hear the swish of my dress from the first time a boy asked me to dance.

More often than not, the wine is dry, just like that time I don't like to talk about but sometimes still cry about. I much prefer a wet trauma, because once you choke it down it's over but a dry trauma lingers on your tongue like the words to a story that you want to tell but can't.

See, I think the truth is that a poet is just like a wine connoisseur in that we cannot just leave well enough alone. We have to uncork at some point and sip on our trauma years later to remember how it tasted.

A poet, like a wine connoisseur, must learn to appreciate the bitterness because a fine vintage is best shared.

A poet, unlike a wine connoisseur, cannot taste just a sip or spit out the mouthful after picking apart its components.

A poet, unlike a wine connoisseur, must drink the whole bottle.

# 4. KARMA, OR WORSE

I hope wherever you are, you are getting the day you deserve. I've no idea if you think of me often, if you remember my face, if you can still look yourself in the mirror, but I sure hope it's cold wherever you are.

Lady Justice is blind, as it were, but so is Nemesis. Isn't it funny, how alike they look?

I only pray to one of them.

Those scales she holds sure look heavy. I'm offering to help hold them for her- you should respect your elders, you know?

They say the quickest way to hell is by holding hate in your heart. If that's the case, then I'll just be here, tending the fire and waiting for you. Don't worry too much about me- the Furies and I are old friends.

Mother says I should practice Forgiveness, but I don't know her. I never did.

I think that sometimes, it is ok to just be angry.

# 5. HERCULES WAS AN ASSHOLE

Hercules was an asshole.

Don't be blinded by an 8-pack and a jawline, sweetheart.

See the cliché lion tattoo for "strength" as the red flag that it is (I'm pretty sure the Nemean lion didn't ask to be slain).

We don't trust gym rats who've been strangling snakes since birth (go ask Medusa how she feels about that- I don't imagine she's into hair pulling).

His twelve-step fitness routine includes ogling Hippolyta's ass, before dumbbell curls and after squats.

All it took was another woman driving him mad for him to forget all about Megara (in some versions of the story, he kills her and their children and makes the front page of the newspaper. We never questioned the bruises before now).

How funny it is that Hera gets the blame.

Funny how easy it was to bring the world's strongest hero to his knees.

Funny how that part wasn't in the movie.

# 6. YOU DON'T DESERVE MY POEMS

Sometimes when I try to write about you, I press my pen so hard against the paper that it breaks and the ink bleeds.

There is a metaphor I could draw there, but I don't want to. I don't have anything else to write about you today.

You don't deserve my ink.

You never did.

# 7. POSEIDON'S FOLLY

I was always going to be the Athena to your Poseidon.

You tried to make me your sea queen, as if the ocean could contain all of me. Did you think casting me aside could break me into smaller pieces? Would you leave space for your new Amphitrite?

You'll make Gorgons out of all your new lovers who try to fill what you'll realize will always remain my temple (Don't think they can't see my image graffitied everywhere)- though I'll leave it empty, since you've desecrated it, and I do not forgive.

Oh, but did you think I would leave you our old friends, to comfort you in your sorrow? Remember, Poseidon, who the Athenians chose in the end. Maybe you can fill your spring with your sorrows.

I may have made the Olive Tree, but it will keep its branches. I am not suing for peace.

Do not forget, Sea King- War is also my domain.

# 8. NICKELS AND DIMES

When you first dropped me from your pocket like a nickel you didn't value enough to get down on your hands and knees in the middle of the dirty parking lot to search for because the kind of girl that you wanted was a dime a dozen but I was only half that-

I started biting my lips.

And no, I don't mean in a cute way, not in the way that a girl does when she is a siren beckoning you to her. Not in the way she might bite her lip while looking you directly in the eyes after pulling a lollipop out of her mouth (yes, we've all been there, I know those tricks; why do you think they call it a sucker?).

I mean in a savage way, a rip-the-skin-off-with-your-teeth kind of way, like peeling an onion's layers until your eyes start to water and you taste copper because I know you always liked me in my war paint, red lipstick and a little black dress, but this time I want to taste the blood, this time I want to remove the flesh with violence and peel off every layer that ever rested against your mouth while you swore forever against my teeth.

You liked them the color of cherries so this time I will demand the blood from them garnet like my birthstone because this is a rebirth.

Didn't you know?

This is a new life and I'm tearing my way in just like the first time, gasping and blood covered and screaming, with brand new lips raw and chapped but wholly mine because they will have never touched yours.

One day, someone will look down and see not a dime or a nickel but a lucky penny.

They won't be afraid to kneel down in the dirty parking lot as if in the church pews at prayer and when that day comes-

I swear I'll bite my lips for all the right reasons instead.

# 9. YOU SHOULD WATCH A K-DRAMA, YOU MIGHT LEARN SOMETHING

In every K-drama I've ever watched, the girl gets hit by the speeding car, the boy running to her just a bit late. Or, to her broken form right on time.

Listen, in the summer we jumped from cliffs, one at a time, never holding hands. Once, you went first and you touched rock with your foot, calling back a warning that could not have stopped me from following even if it had been spoken sooner. Before the fall. I never was any good at looking before leaping.

Somewhere, Patroclus still dons the armor. Somewhere, Icarus still takes flight. Somewhere, the boy cradles her body and begs her not to leave.

We do not wonder why she faced down the oncoming vehicle instead of moving aside (we all know what happens when doe eyes look to the light).

In Florida, I swam out in the ocean past the pier alone because you would not get in the water with me. I turned back to look for you and saw a fin slip beneath the waves a few hundred yards away. When I finally made it back to the sand, gasping, you told me "Don't worry, I was watching you."

I wondered how you had planned to save me from the shore.

# 10. SWIMMING IN THE LETHE

You have become an idea that I've chased after in so many different faces that I've lost count. I can't even talk about the blue oceans in your eyes because I can't remember if they were brown earth more recently. I've taken all the hurt you gave and forged it into a weapon against those new who've tried to love me, wanting it to be you that I was hurting but really just bleeding over everything, like always.

You liked me quiet and I liked me lonely.

I think you fantasized about loving a ghost girl like me but let's be honest, you just wanted a fuck toy and I was all too happy to be that for you. Until I wasn't, and then you left, and it was me feeling like I loved a ghost boy.

Ghost boy, incorporeal, you managed to slip through my fingers like water only after you made sure that you were the air I breathed and honestly I think you just liked watching me drown on you.

Is that why you used to choke me during sex? Or did you just want me quiet that badly?

I can't remember if you ever loved me. I can't remember if I ever loved you.

They say ignorance is bliss, but I can't remember if that's true.

# 11. MEDUSA MAKES A MISTAKE

I didn't realize what was happening until I smelled the ocean in your hair and tasted the salt.

"It was just three drinks, just three drinks" I plead to Dionysus, over and over, as if that mantra would erase you pushing into me, over and over.

My inner goddess, in disgust, purges my stomach, over and over. She can't stand the sight of me in the mirror.

(Have I sprouted scales? Is that me hissing when someone moved too close?)

I was never a priestess.

Just a stupid girl, drunk.

Left alone with a boy, drunk.

Athena's punishment seems just.

I shouldn't have trusted him so much.

## 12. WHEN RECONCILING GREEKS AND ROMANS, KEEP YOUR EYES ON MARS

You terrify me.

Not because you are Ares, but because I am Bellona and I've just realized that I am not your Aphrodite.

I may stand at your side, hold your spear, hold your shield, but I've never held your heart.

I wonder if it tastes like blood?

# 13. OUT-MONSTERING A MONSTER

When my loved ones ask me why  I stopped taking such good care of myself-

[Honey, you don't look so good- what happened?]

What I wish I'd said was "After my third lover, who used me like an eraser (that is to say, like the kind that you stick over the wound on the end of your pencil and use to grind your mistakes to nothing over and over again until you get be up with streaks of grime on your page and then throw the eraser away like the mess was its fault all along and only then does the boy decide to turn to a clean page), I decided that maybe I was better off twisting my body into this grotesque thing that I could wear like armor against future invasions."

What I wish I'd said was "I will shed my skin like a snake if it means not feeling the fingerprints of those who've touched it. I will out-monster the monsters who would have come next. Not unlike Lilith, I will spawn demons before I let Adam lay on top of me. Unlike Eve, I will banish myself from the Garden. The Lord says my body is a temple, and I would rather be a forgotten deity turned to rubble before letting false worshippers desecrate me again."

What I wish I'd said was "My bones hurt and there is this ancient ache in my chest and sometimes my knees pop so loud it startles me."

What I wish I'd said was "I don't really sleep anymore and I think at this point a tattoo would be less permanent than the bags under my eyes."

What I actually said was "I'm just tired."

[Drink some water, Honey, you look dehydrated!]

# 14. THE DEFINITION OF INSANITY

I am Alice chasing endlessly after a white rabbit that smells an awful lot like whiskey until I dive down down the rabbit hole and wind up in you again.

Note, I did not say fall, I said dive.

See, falling is an accident but diving is a choice and I choose to go head first off the deep end.

My heart is labeled "Eat Me", "Drink Me", "Use Me", "Consume Me".

I will make your ego grow and your hurt shrink- at least for a while.

Long enough for you to forget yourself, for a while. Long enough to forget her, for a while.

See, I am not your red queen, you already have your queen of hearts and I'd offer my head to her on the chopping block over and over and over again if it would make you happy.

See, I was not made for the tea party or to be in your wonderland, but I will be your sacrificial lamb, your knave, your pawn, and each time until wonderland decides to stop playing it's mad mad games with me.

# 15. HERA SHOULD DIVORCE HIM

"Smile, baby," loud as a thunderclap from across the street.

I'm not much for smiling, so I show him my fangs.

This I know how to do.

You call your wife your Queen and your house your Castle, and still make time to harass girls walking home.

Listen up, he-who-would-be-King: I'm not a girl, I'm the Masses. I'm the Rebellion, and now I'm screaming for your head on a pike.

Zeus, babe, did you forget about your own father?

Let's find out what happens when your god-complex meets the devil herself.

# 16. HAVE YOU EVER TRIED DANDELION TEA?

The hurt grows in my garden like a particularly stubborn weed. When I reach my hands down into the dirt to rip you out by the roots, more and more of the carefully compressed topsoil flies away with the wind.

There, a root exposed. The time you held me in your arms until I fell asleep, sobbing my heartbreak into your shirt.

Here, a stem accidentally snapped. You filling my car with antifreeze in the cold because fuck if I know anything about car maintenance.

A leaf ripped in half. Moving me out of my apartment, carrying all the heavy boxes singlehandedly.

Petals crushed underfoot. Buying all my drinks, a palm on my waist and a pointed glare my shield against the boys at the bar with their hands prone to wandering.

Fertilizer spilled from the bag. Your eyes staring into mine.

A bruised plant. Your eyes staring into mine.

Crushed seeds. Your eyes staring into mine.

Did you know that most weeds are just herbs growing under the wrong circumstances?

I'm going to salt this earth. Nothing will grow here again.

# 17. OPHELIA CHOSE HER FATE

Do you think that I drowned in that river, Hamlet? Let me tell you a secret- Icarus and I have more in common than you think.

A sprig of purple columbine for you, my dear.

The Fates cannot control you if you cut your own thread. I am not a suicidal damsel, my love. I am a Naiad, and I jumped from the willow to my sisters' embrace.

I didn't need your crown- one of violets waited for me beneath the water.

If I am to be the Lady of the Lake, deciding Kinghood, then I will return to the water because I choose myself. There is no Camelot waiting for you. Excalibur is mine. Lady Macbeth's only mistake was letting someone else sit upon her throne.

You might rue the day you met me, but I left my regrets on the shore.

Here, I can dance among the daisies again.

I suppose there is a certain madness in rejecting destiny-

But god, what freedom.

# 18. YOU CAN KEEP YOUR MR. DARCY; I WANTED HEATHCLIFF

Growing up, my sister and I were overly fond of Bronte novels.

This should come as no surprise from little girls who read before they talked and drank tea in treehouses.

She always favored Pride and Prejudice, but my story read more like Wuthering Heights. I liked my men tall, dark, and brooding.

I take my tea with two lumps of spite and a splash of bitterness.

Call me Cathy, if you like, but isn't that what happens to little girls in love with Heathcliff?

(I should have seen this one coming.)

# 19. HE GREW GILLS, NOT WINGS

The myths don't tell you this: Apollo let Icarus fall.

Is there a worse rejection than two burnt wings and a drowning?

The myths don't tell you this: Icarus was made for the sea.

He just couldn't see that with the sun in his eyes.

# 20. HELL HATH NO FURY

Medea could teach us a thing or two about a spiteful woman.

Of course, we blame her.

Murderess- her gift to the world was sevenfold what the world gave to her.

Should we wonder at the mania of a woman, driven to kill?

Why do we still call Jason "hero"?

Isn't it funny how Hercules has his own movie and soundtrack while Medea is a warning? Megara's ghost still holds her dead children and wonders why.

I thought we reviled the tempter? The snake in the garden is more hated than the tempted Eve, surely?

Perhaps we could all learn something from a woman who teaches the world her pain.

Medea knew what it takes for a woman to survive to the end of the story.

# 21. LET ME TEACH YOU ABOUT THIRST

I know thirst better than a desert knows drought.

What I mean is my soul has been so long deprived of you that I no longer recognize myself as entirely human. The split ends of this red thread are so flayed that even Zeus isn't sure if I was ever whole.

What I mean is that the gaping wound carved out of this chest in the shape of you has rotted, twisted, warped, that you would no longer fit even if you tried.

This is what moisture does to wood over time, I am told

Who cares if the glass is half empty or half full if you no longer recognize that you are supposed to drink it?

Parched is too soft a sentiment- try empty, try lacking, try missing.

Try incomplete.

I can't seem to get past this lump of salt in my throat- it is all that I have left of the sea after it dried up inside me.

Too much seawater is bad for you, right?

I think salt and dehydration burn my throat the same.

Tastes a bit like vodka, if I'm honest, which I never am. They say I drink like a fish anyway, so who can blame me if I sucked the river dry?

It's never enough. Let me teach you about thirst.

Who are you again?

I think I knew you, once.

# 22. DO YOU THINK MACHIAVELLI WAS LONELY?

Listen, do you think Machiavelli was lonely?

When he wrote "it is better to be feared than loved", do you think he was in mourning?

Who was not brave enough to love him?

Do you think God wept in the same way after Lucifer was cast out of Heaven?

Listen, I know it is 2 AM and I should be asleep but do parents not still love their children when they rebel?

Lucifer was the Morning Star and the most beautiful of the angelic host and frankly it took me ages to throw away my favorite dress after it stopped fitting. But the Bible is filled with "hate the sin, not the sinner"- do you think this was the first evidence of divine regret?

Do you think Jesus wished that Judas feared him more, or loved him better?

Listen, it came to me in the shower that I just can't think of an act of greater devotion than washing someone else's feet and I just don't understand a love that loves you more than themselves, I never did, but I think I'm in good company.

And maybe I'm a bit too wine drunk to be pondering the nature of betrayal but wasn't that exactly what the philosophers did?

Do you think they needed to be drunk for that conversation?

Could God still look Michael in the eyes after the war?

Was thirteen pieces of silver really worth it?

How many times do the Psalms sing of fearing the Lord?

Listen, do you think Machiavelli was lonely?

# 23. SEAMSTRESS

I never learned how to work a sewing machine, but I am particularly good at mending torn holes and frayed edges.

Think Arachne before the Spider legs.

I think I love the same way I sew- trying to stitch back together the broken parts like Frankenstein stitched the flesh of his monster until I can give back the mended garment- an ugly scar where the hole used to be, perhaps, but the thread strong and the tear completely closed.

My patrons don't stay longer than it takes me to sew up the hole and leave with no thanks but ready to meet the world fully clothed, as Adam emerging from the Garden.

I think I am also loved the way I sew.

No matter how careful the stitch or how lovingly weaved the patch, no one stays for the final tie of the knot.

# 24. AMPHITRITE TAKES BACK THE SEA

I remember the ways in which you tried to convince me of your divinity. The tidal laughs, the sparkling eyes.

I wove a crown of shells and named you Earthshaker, God of the Sea, content to lap around your ankles as seafoam kisses the coast.

Years later, I stand facing a different ocean, my arms raised to push the tangled strands of hair off my face, feeling more like seaweed than I've ever felt.

I remember all the times I dragged you to the beach, through storms and through sun, wading into the ocean while you stayed on shore.

"I don't like the cold water", you used to tell me when I'd beg you to join me dancing in the waves.

I wonder how I could have ever forgotten that I, too, am divine.

The sea was always my home, and I am not sharing that anymore.

You can't take what does not belong to you.

# 25. STOP LOOKING FOR A HERO

You like your men with back muscles of Atlas.

That is to say, you like your men strong enough to carry the weight of your heart but oh, my dear, when Atlas puts down the sky your whole world falls.

Darling, this is a lesson on loving a man like a myth.

Remember, dear, that men are mortal too- do not demand ichor from their veins. To do so is a form of cruelty too; let them be flesh and bone. Let them be man, without demanding a demigod- lest you make a monster of man instead.

Darling, Atlas was never going to be able to hold all the love you had to give.

[I know you are scared that no one will but they will, I promise]

Your blue eyes reminded him of the sky, but please don't get it confused; he was never lost in your gaze- the sky was his burden to carry, remember?

[Note, darling, you are not a burden]

Sky girl, don't you dare pull your head out of the clouds, though the world may scream that you are easier to love with your feet planted. Thunder and pour if you must [as we all must], but never apologize for the rain.

The man who can hold the weight of your heart will make you feel weightless.

His arms will not be an anchor to tether you to the ground so that you don't rise too far above him.

His arms were made to lift you high.

# 26. POCKETS

As a child, my mother always made me turn out my pockets at the door.

Out would come tumbling rocks & leaves & feathers-

See, even then, I liked to pick things up. My hands were made for carrying things with me. Even now, years later, all my clothes still have pockets.

Only now, in adulthood, I learned to carry heartache & anxiety & the emotions of strangers-

I tuck them away into the pockets of my dress; except now, there is no one standing at the door telling me to put it down before I go inside.

They say, as you grow older, you'll open your mouth one day and your mother's voice will come out. "Darling, empty those pockets. You cannot bring these things home."

(I guess that part of adulthood means picking up responsibility, too.)

As I stand here, unloading my pockets and tossing these less necessary items away from me before I allow myself to step foot over the threshold of my being, the poems start to come easier.

The poems start to come easier, now, and I wonder if this is what happiness feels like- a sigh, a deep breath, and letting things go.

My hands still shake but no longer from clenching my fists too tightly around the things I pick up but cannot put down.

My hands still shake but at least now they are open.

 My hands still shake but it no longer scares me.

 Darling, unclench your fist. Drop the hurt you've been clutching so tightly.

Release.

This is not giving up.

This is what victory looks like.

# 27. PROMETHEUS WONDERS WHY NICE GUYS FINISH LAST

Prometheus was a nice guy. Of course he was! He brought her gifts, fire, light. He brought her pretty jewelry, civilization, shaped her into something he could recognize and love, right? It's understandable, how angry he was at her rejection, right? His kindness, his gifts- they should have merited some reward, right? No, instead that bitch breaks his heart, like talons in his chest. It's her fault he has to drink himself to sleep every night, right? He'll probably kill his liver this way, and then won't she just feel terrible for rejecting him?

Here's what Prometheus actually brought her: the attention of the gods. And oh, what fun games they are going to play with their new favorite toy.

She didn't ask for any of this. Prometheus, she didn't ask to be burnt.

Perhaps she was better off before you.

# 28. HELEN IS OF SPARTA, FIRST

Helen laughed as Troy burned. Let this be a lesson to every Paris who tries to take.

Helen grinned as the Greeks died in droves. Let this be a lesson to every Menelaus who tries to claim.

Helen chuckled as the gods trembled. Let this be a lesson to those who forget the kind of woman that Sparta calls princess.

Helen was winning games of battleship and cutting the heads off her dolls long before her face launched any ships. Lust is a man's game; Bloodlust is hers.

Helen smirked when the world was brought to heel. Let this be a lesson on the kind of woman that little girls who play with matches grow up to be.

## 29. HOW I LEARNED TO DO THINGS FOR MYSELF

When I came home with the word 'enough' tattooed in morse code over my Achilles tendon, you told me that you didn't "get it".

That's ok, I replied.

It wasn't meant for you.

# 30. WHAT THE OCEAN TAUGHT ME ABOUT SELF LOVE

As I stood on the shore, alone at night, the sea beckoned me with her waves crashing high as far out as I could see in the dark.

"I'm here," I told her.

Come closer.

"I can go no further. There are monsters in your depths that would tear me, rip me, drown me. Swallow me whole".

I never forgot about Jonah.

I know. She smiled.

We are the same.

But you love me anyway, right?

I remember a clam shell, sea foam, pearls.

If Aphrodite can be born of the sea, so can I.